GHOST ARMIES

GHOST ARMIES

FUKUOKA || THE WAIT-A-WHILE VINE

ANDREW SNEDDON

[Lacuna]

2012

All enquiries to the publisher: general@lacunapublishing.com

Published in 2012 by Lacuna
   http://www.lacunapublishing.com

   Lacuna is an imprint of Golden Orb Creative
   PO Box 185, Westgate NSW 2048, Australia
   http://www.goldenorbcreative.com

   Cover design by Golden Orb Creative
   Text layout by Golden Orb Creative
   Typeset in 11/13.2 Palatino and 16/19.2 Optima

National Library of Australia Cataloguing-in-Publication entry

   Sneddon, Andrew
   Ghost armies: Fukuoka; The wait-a-while vine / Andrew
   Sneddon

   ISBN 9781922198006 (pbk.)

   Australian poetry

   Sneddon, Andrew. Ghost Armies [electronic resource].
   Sneddon, Andrew. Fukuoka.
   Sneddon, Andrew. Wait-a-while vine.

   A821.4

CONTENTS

The Wait-a-While Vine

FUKUOKA

Author's Note and Acknowledgements

My great-uncles Wally and Alf Wilder were captured by the Japanese at the fall of Singapore in 1942. They spent time at Changi before being transported to Fukuoka in Japan, where they worked in the coal mines. Alf survived. Wally died of pneumonia a few months before the end of the war.

Slightly different versions of some of the poems have been published previously. Rural arts journal *Coppertales* published 'How I Remember my Brother' as 'Backyard Warriors'. Literary journal *LiNQ* (*Literature in North Queensland*) published 'Beyond the Wire' as 'Snapshot, Iran' and 'Kindness' as 'Roadkill'.

The text of 'Eyewitness' is a slightly modified quote from an account of one of Wally's beatings taken from *The Story of J-Force* by Alexander Dandie (a self-published work of non-fiction).

The five lines quoted at the end of 'Souvenir' are from 'In the Long Run' by Ella Wheeler Wilcox.

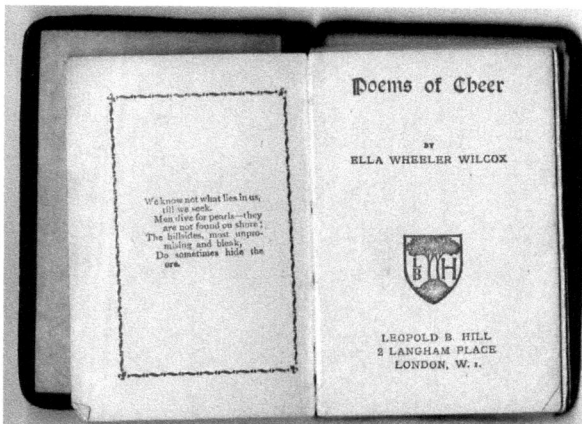

Earlstone Warwick ('Wally') Wilder on enlistment.

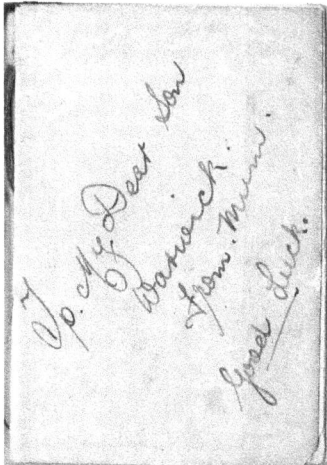

Prison hospital, Thailand, 1942

Flies buzz in the heavy heat
Rounding and dipping at my pursed lips
But I'm too feeble to resist them.
They're warm and tickle-footed in the corners of
    my eyes.
Relentless black energy in a room of weariness.

Mother, I want to put down the load.

I raise myself onto my elbows
For a few seconds
Late in the afternoon
And take in the length of my body.
Light falls through the leaves outside.
I'm patch-worked.
Spindly legs lie in parallels
To the foot of my stretcher
And I cry because I'm so thin
And filthy.

Tropical ulcers.

O Mother, forgive me,
Dying is so easy.

Prison transport, Changi To Fukuoka, Japan, 1943

They bullied us into the hold
And screwed the hatch closed
On their shouts and chatter topside.
We panted in the foul air
Dreading an American torpedo.

There was no light for days.
My brother sitting by my side
Was a tense, humid presence
Slippery with perspiration.

There were sobs from in the dark.

From time to time
A man ten feet from me
Would strike a match
And check his watch.

Fifty desperate pairs of eyes
Would turn and stare.

In the smothering darkness
The point of flame
Was like a nail in a wall
That an unhinged man
Could hang a picture on.

Fukuoka

Worse by far
Than hot and hungry

Is cold and hungry.

Alighting, Japan, 1943

Even the gentler guards were kicking us
And shrieking like maniacs.

The locals turned out for the show,
Lining the platform
And then the streets
To hiss and spit
As we hobbled past.

I was in a dirty shirt
And tattered Changi loincloth.

There were dreadful beatings.
The women sneered at us.
The children gathered stones
From the roadside
And hurled them at our bony arses.
Ah, the conquering heroes.

And what right of reply?

I kept my head down.
With my frightened dick
Cringing tiny beneath my lap-lap
Even an angry sideways glance
Would have seemed, to all of us,
More than a little absurd.

First night

It was different then.
There was no Hiroshima.
No 1945.
It was just the beginning of something horrible
That could go on forever.

Prisoners of war

Mostly fetid stillness
And an occasional slick spasm of resentment

Like slimy carp in a diminishing pond-pool
Writhing against a weir.

Signing up

When my father got it in the neck in 1917
Crockery rattled in the kitchen
Of a tiny terrace house in Redfern.
Black lace doily'd a bewildered widow.

The evening that the news came through
Saw us three small children
Asking for dinner at tea-time
Like it was any other day.
My mother *wailed*.

Not quite comprehending
We cried ourselves to sleep that night
Sensing, correctly, a colossal shift.

Off civvy street

Wally and I joined up together in '40 –
Two brothers.
It was the done thing.

My mother paled when we sauntered into the
       kitchen –
Our uniforms and slouch hats,
And our rude boots
Scuffing black into her nice clean linoleum.

Adversaries

We signed up to fight the Germans
Like our parents had.

We hadn't even thought about the Japs
Who at the time
Might have seemed to us
Somewhat beneath our dignity.

Proving grounds

I recall reeling hard against
A snag beneath the surface,
Bending the rod with
A child's thin-lipped determination.

When the line snapped
Sending a whisper of thread
Curling like a burnt hair
Over the river

Dad stepped up to me
And took the rod from my hands.
He slipped the handline
Into my palm.

The one for women and tiddlers.

Mum

On the day we shipped out
She took me aside
When my brother wasn't looking.

She said:
Look after Wally will you?

I. Grudges

I have noticed that the infant's soft hand,
By some primordial reflex,
Will close involuntarily around a finger
Or lock of hair.
Snatching and the clenched fist
Are ours by instinct.

Opening the palm is a learned gesture.

Invasion

Invasion is a narrowed man
Half rubbed out.
A face smeared sideways.
A distillate reeking of ditch water.

It is a man-thing dragged from a roadside channel
With one arm bent stiffly across the chest,
The other rigid by his side,
Legs curled like a foetus kinked at the hip.

Invasion is
One wit joking
That they could make a fortune
Hiring his withered arse out
To horny soldiers four weeks on the peninsula.
And it is everybody laughing.

And it is the dog finding it irresistible –
His dainty shy licking,
His cool wet nose nuzzling the creased leather-flesh,
And him having a go at it
Before anyone could stop him.
(Dragged it three feet before they shoo'd him away.)

It is the dog grinning and bounding and wagging
        its tail,
Joining in the fun,
Keen for another go
In next to
No time
At all.

I. Cruelty

Gold Tooth –
Who beat us worse than any of them –
Was a market gardener before the war.

He grew tomatoes.

II. Cruelty

Does it give him a hard-on?
Does it stiffen him up?
Does he return to barracks
And toss off under the blankets?

Brother

I'm worried about my brother.
He carries himself too tall.

They beat him more than most of us
Because he forgets to feel humiliated.

Fukuoka winter

No part of a woman is as soft as this –

My tepid penis in the cold morning
Pissing steam out of the ground.

Burial, 1917

Poor Dad.

I imagine a lull –
A sudden peculiar ceasing of the guns –
And the sound of shovels
Going to work in the stillness.

I've buried a few myself now.
A shovel plunging into the loam
Sounds like a gasp of surprise.

III. Cruelty

A cruel man will set himself
Above your cowering body,
Position and re-position his stance,
And *then* swing the stick.

He takes time to find the pain for you.
The white rub of the ankle bone,
The round knuckle of the wrist,
The elegantly curved collar bone.

And your balls of course.
He'll aim for your balls
And laugh.

How I remember my brother

The whir of cicadas lends a bogus urgency
To the scone-dry heat.
Over the fence and in the house
It's ennui and lethargy.

We are Cowboys and Indians
War-whooping in the backyard –
Quick draws on the pop guns
And keen on extravagant deaths –
Brave warriors disdaining warm milk,
Determined to camp in the cubby house 'til dawn
But coming at dusk when beckoned from the hot
        back-step:

  C'mon kids. That'll do.
  Come and get your dinner.

I can still hear her
And the squeaky fly-screen slamming at our backs
As they fade into dark interiors.

Note: This poem was published in slightly different form as
'Backyard Warriors' in the journal Coppertales.

II. Grudges

Only dogs will forgive without rancour.
Closer to their elemental stuff
They understand the basic impersonality
Of sudden cruelty.

Taking life

I wasn't looking for him.

It was before my capture.
He stalked into my sights
From behind a banana tree
And I killed him with a single shot.

Was he a deep thinker?

Frugality

Vic Paterson of Drummoyne
Had his arm crushed in a mine collapse
And died of gangrene three weeks later.

A former barrack-mate,
I helped to bury him.
As we lowered his tiny body into the grave
I noticed in his face that something was awry –
They'd taken his false teeth out.

He'd have hated that,
And two days later
The shambling Oklahoman
With a new wide smile.

A beating

Gold Tooth laid into me one day
With a bamboo stick.
I could tell he wasn't serious
And took the blows
Bent around my knees,
Hands over my soft skull.

One, two, three, four.
I counted them off in my head
And glimpsing his split-toed sandals
Could think of nothing better
Than a man with his
Undies wedged up his arse.

Despair

I have forgotten all their names –
The dead ones, I mean.
But it doesn't matter.
When I am gone forget mine too.

I'm worthless.

Lessons

Will I grow old?

The young need to be reminded
That the suffering of others
And at another time

Is at least the equal
Of their petty miseries.

Gold Tooth

The awesome potential of his laugh.

Loose-jawed and snorty
Like a big dog wrestling.

My brother

How many years without a mirror?

Wally's rubbing a dry patch on his chin.
He turns to me and asks:
Can you see anything?

He's making himself vulnerable,
Saying:
Here, find my flaws.

Hierarchies

The youngest died first
And then the oldest.

And always,
The unlucky.

III. Grudges

The pink-cheeked and gurgling infant,
Replete at the mother's breast,
Will test its emerging teeth
On the big, brown, tantalising nipple.

A cry of pain and a mouthful of rich warm milk.

The child will remember only the nutriment.

Body and soul

I've admired more than my fair share
Of crimson sunsets
Resting on my heels,
Chin uptilted,
Voiding into the shitter.

Beyond the wire

Pumped water,
Cool and clear-eyed,
Gushing from the fountainhead.

She must lean carefully
On slippery rocks to reach it.
She makes a cupid's bow of her lips
And gently kisses the skin of the flow.

She's bent a little at the waist.
She closes her eyes.

*Note: This poem was previously published in slightly
different form as 'Snapshot' in the journal LiNQ.*

Indifference

We called the tiny punishment cell
The dog box.
Timber roof, walls and floors.

Wally spent seven days and nights in it once
For giving lip
And returned to barracks afterwards
Looking weary
With the wood-grain impressed
Into one pinked cheek.

But in the dog box
Where he suffered –
Not a dent,
Not a chip,
Not a mark.

The mine

Sometimes the rock squeaks
Like glass twisting
And all our picks fall silent
In a panicked instant.

But if the rock face were to sheer away
And if I were buried beneath
The weight of the mountain

Would I amount to a lump of coal?

Bombast

The second thing I'm going to do
When I get home
Is take my pack off.

All bluster of course.
As likely as not
They were virgins
At the Fall of Singapore,
And this much is certain –

They've not had much practice since.

I. Memory

One morning,
Six inches of snow!

No mud or shit
But a white stillness
Both light and crisp.

After parade we walked to the mine in silence,
Our wooden clogs stuffed with rags
And crunching into the snow.
It was a strange, muffled suffering.

It was beautiful for three days.

Returning from the mine on the fourth day
Approaching the wretched boggy compound,
I tried to call to my mind the lovely image
Of our whitened camp,

But it had gone.

Locale

Any place may be a venue
For cruelty –

School room,
Church hall,
Wheat field,
Battle field.

It's the people
That bring the evil.

I. Kindness

Uncanny how the dog's frantic wail
Caught the pitch
Of the screeching tyres exactly
And held it.

In pain and a kind of embarrassment
He limped and stumbled from the road
On his three good legs,
Seeking out a warm dark corner
And the delicate, pink-tongued
Lick, lick, lick of self-misery.

At the first awful scream
I saw a big-shouldered builder
Lay down his plasterer's trowel gently.
He walked towards the crying,
His lined face
Softening to tenderness.

*Note: A slightly different version of this poem was published
under the title 'Roadkill' in the journal LiNQ.*

Alchemy

One of the English sappers has pellagra.

I can't bear to look at him.
His skin is puffed and oozy
And his clothes have become a torment.

British, American, Australian –
We were all raised meat and potatoes boys
But we are more *scientific* now about our food.
We know what causes pellagra.
He died of cheap over-polished rice.

Life and death.
There's really not much in it.
Living can be the difference
Between the husk
And the grain.

The abuser and abused

This much we are agreed on –

It is shameful
To be beaten.

Night escape

I rook my nose in the angle made
By the wall and the floor
And lying on my filthy mattress
Flee to a cosy world
The size of two cupped hands.

II. Kindness

The hospital ward is a quiet place.
Birds twitter in the trees
Outside the windowless windows.

Within its walls
Burly men lower their deep voices
And joke softly beside the beds of sick friends.
There are unfussy manly kindnesses.

In one corner
A sailor holds a water bottle
To the lips of a prone patient
Who coughs up more than he swallows.

The carer says:
It's alright, son. Take your time.

Both of them
Not five years out of high school.

II. Memory

The body remembers.

On the coldest nights
When buckets and water troughs
Were glassy with ice

I could sometimes be found
In our drafty barracks
Sweating and ranting
In a tropical delirium.

Two years after Changi
The malaria would return,
Unexpected,
Like an incubated wrong.

Dignity

I think of starved men with schoolboy knees
In baggy too-long shorts.

At morning parade you'd see men reduced to rags,
And a dozen kinds of head gear.
US sailors,
English airmen,
And the slouch hat.

At the order,
Broken down men would stand
At something like attention
And the Japs would laugh
We looked so ridiculous.

But I'd always search the crowd to find them –
The jauntier walks
And the hats at rakish angles.

Anxieties

Four years of starvation and beatings.
What effect does that have on a man?

When it's all over,
How many wives
Will retire to empty beds
Leaving husbands in the kitchen sipping tea
Hunched over formica tabletops?

Death

Not the jealous cat
Eyeing the mistress's newborn
With a cold and passionless stare,

But a scatty, eager-fingered monkey.
A grimace of sharp teeth
And balled fists at the mouth.

Amputee

A quarter of him gone
From hip to sole.
He was as light as a child.

When we told him that the Japs
Might supply us with extra morphine
He grew angry.
He said:

The last thing I want
Is that they should be merciful.

Reflections

The first butter that I ate after the camps
I sicked up on my shirt-front like an infant.
I lost a tooth.
Women made me stutter.

Naked from a shower one morning after liberation
I passed my first full-length mirror in four years
And was startled by a stooped stranger
Who appraised my skinny haunches sorrowfully
From the shadows of a dim room.

But *they* made us this way!
Why were they so cruel?
Did they beat us because we were repulsive?

Overheads

At night the parade ground
Is bled down to white moonlight
And the echo of distant coughs.

Anger is a luxury of calories
That we can ill afford.
At day's end the camp is sluggish
And blanket-huddled.
The value of motion and emotion
Must be measured against rice and watery soup.

When a man dies there is a gentle stirring
From within a few friendly blankets.
Brothers and barrack-mates.
A slow shuffling to the sick bay.

The rest of us must be frugal with our strength.
We are saddened
But quite relaxed now
About death.

Eyewitness

Gold Tooth formed us into line
One behind the other.
I was last.
Wally stood in front of me.
I knew his older brother Alf –
A quiet shy man –
Would be worrying himself sick
As he waited in the barracks.

When Gold Tooth had reached the third man
I had picked up the sequence of the blows –
Right arm, backhand, right, back, right, back
With a Jap composition belt.
He was smiling as he struck
And proceeded down the line.

Back to number one in the line.
This time
A steel ruler.

Six weapons in all.
Number five was a twenty inch length of hose pipe.
The last was a kendo sword stick
With which Gold Tooth finished with a flourish.
A blow crashing down on the forehead,
Next the right side of the face
Then the left.
Repeated three times.

The Japs dispersed,
Well-pleased.

Wally and I walked silently
And with burning faces
To our barracks
Where some of the lads
Stood at their doors.
Alf followed Wally into his room.
Roy queried, 'OK mate?'
I just nodded.

Note: 'Eyewitness' is adapted from an account of one of Wally's
beatings in The Story of J-Force by Alexander Dandie.

Pneumonia

I can hear Wally's wet breathing in the darkness.
Many hours after taking to bed
It occurs to me that he may be dying.

The winter night has become
A dull unrelenting ache.
I have one thin blanket
Greasy with two years of my own
Exertions and clammy fevers.

Wally needs it.
And I need it.

I pull the blanket over my head
Like a child
And look for warmth in my own fug.
As dawn approaches
We curl around the cold stones in our bellies,
Side by side,
Like opposing question marks.

The turning tide

A bow drawn across a taut string.
Thrumming bass note of the cello.

We dare not look
But we can hear
A squadron of friendly bombers
Passing in the dawn gloom.

They can't stop themselves.
The guards tilt their heads back
And squint their eyes.

A mild man at the worst of times,
I think of flimsy rice-paper cities
And the scalding flame
And descend exultantly into our black mine.

Honour roll

Men with silly names –
Percival, Reginald, Cyril and Wally –
Dying of such *serious* things!

More friendly bombers, 1945

We could smell the smoke
Of their burning cities.

Lying on my mattress at night
I drew pleasure from the irony

That the drone of the bombers' engines
Shared its tone with a Shinto chant.

I. Liberation

Who would have thought that I'd come to think of it
       as home!
On the first morning
We woke to find
That they had opened the gates for us in the night,
But we were too scared to walk through them.

Forgetting we were free
We glimpsed the outside world
For the first few hours
From between familiar gateposts.
I only passed through them in the afternoon
When the bravest of us had come back drunk.

Obsequious guards
Bowed and beamed as we exited,
Leaving me feeling hurt and perplexed.

Looking back from outside the wire
I could see clusters of uncertain men
Peering out,
Paused,
Waiting for life,

And a laundry of rags behind my barracks
Flapping in the breeze,
Like us,
Threadbare.

II. Liberation

In spite of the fantasies
There were no orgies of violence.
No revenge.
It was enough to know we'd won

And to see the women in the village
Flee from us in panic,
Dragging their daughters
Out of sight and away
From the dark potential in our trousers.

After

Like a dog that whets its teeth
On a stripped bone
Long after the flesh is gone
I'd lie on my mattress at night
And gnash my teeth on the memory.

Anzac Day in old age

I used to be one for hunting –
Rabbits mainly,
And nuisance roos –
But guns don't interest me now.

I'm content to leave the rabbits to the myxo.
Disease or a bullet.
They both will do the job.

Before the war we'd flush them out with dogs
And get them as they scampered
For their burrows.
I don't do that any more.
That rabbit breaking cover
And careering across the dust
Was me a few times.

I've gone soft with age.
I'm funny about guns.
I've never been to the marches.
It seems to me that there are too many weapons

And always in the air
The smell of sun-warmed gun metal.
Salty,
Like blood.

Tally

It weighs on me

But there were worse men than I was.
As far as I'm aware
I killed just one man in the war.

Two if you count Wally.

Souvenir

The day we buried Wally
The doctor gave me a bound book
With a weathered leather cover,
Smaller than a child's palm,
Found in his pocket.

It was called *Poems of Cheer*
And on the inside cover
My mother had written:
To My Dear Son Warwick.
From Mum.
Good Luck.
The last two words, underlined.

The first poem
Was called 'In the Long Run':

> *In the long run goodly sorrows pay.*
> *There is no better thing than righteous pain!*
> *The sleepless nights, the awful thorn-crowned days,*
> *Bring sure reward to tortured soul and brain …*
> *In the long run.*

IV. Grudges

The Japs?
You know,
I never really hated them.

But I never really liked them much either.

THE WAIT-A-WHILE VINE

Historical Note

In May 1848 a party of thirteen explorers landed in Rockingham Bay, midway between where Cairns and Townsville are now situated, with the intention of travelling overland to Port Albany, a tiny settlement on the northern tip of Cape York Peninsula.

The expedition was well provisioned – 28 horses, 100 sheep, three carts, and tons of flour, sugar and other supplies – and it was under the leadership of a young but experienced explorer named Edmund Besley Court Kennedy. However, the expedition proved to be a disaster. By December 1848 all but three of the men were dead, including Kennedy who was speared to death by the local Aboriginal inhabitants within sight of a rescue ship waiting at anchor at Port Albany.

Kennedy was a handsome Englishman, born in 1818 into a comfortable family on Guernsey in the Channel Islands. His father was an army colonel and once a mayor of London. But Kennedy was taken with surveying as a young man and in 1840 he had settled in Sydney, where he became an Assistant-Surveyor to the colony. He cut a dashing figure in the city's small social scene, but he also earned a reputation for his ability as a surveyor, accompanying Sir Thomas Mitchell in his exploration of Central Australia, especially along the Barcoo River. By the time Kennedy landed in Rockingham Bay he had years of experience behind him. He was not expected to encounter too many difficulties.

In fact, his expedition struck trouble from the start. One horse was drowned in the landing. Then, meeting with impenetrable rainforest and scrub, the men had to travel southwards for weeks – away from their intended destination – before they could strike inland and then northwards again. Hacking through the tangle of forest, hampered by the 'lawyer' or 'wait-a-while' vines,[1] they lost half their sheep in the first six weeks, as well as valuable time. Inland, the going was little easier, with the scrublands proving difficult territory to traverse. The men and animals grew weak and ill. The local traditional owners – initially friendly – turned hostile and harried the expedition for most of the trek, at times lighting scrub fires to frustrate the explorers. The carts were abandoned. Morale dropped. Men began stealing the precious food. And one man deserted (returning later after living for a time with the Aboriginal people in the area).

An indispensable member of the team was a young Aboriginal man – Jacky Jacky – whose bushcraft and strength proved invaluable. He was most likely from the Hunter Valley in New South Wales, and he didn't know the Aboriginal languages of North Queensland. He was unfamiliar with much of the local flora. He was as much a stranger in North Queensland as Kennedy and the white men were.

The expedition fell badly behind schedule so Kennedy decided to divide the party. He left eight men at a camp near Weymouth Bay under the leadership of Mr Carron, the expedition botanist, while he pressed on with the remaining four men in the hope of catching the rescue ship – the *Ariel* – far to the north where a rendezvous had been arranged. However, in mid-November matters deteriorated further when one of the men accidentally shot himself while unloading his saddle bags. Kennedy left the wounded man with the

---

1   A species of Calamus vine, so-called because its thorns get their hooks into you, and force you to wait while you unhook yourself.

other two men, while he and Jacky made a desperate dash for the *Ariel* alone.

Weakened by hunger and harried by Aboriginal tribesmen, Kennedy and Jacky struggled through the scrub for the coast. From the top of a hill shaped like an upturned pudding pan[2] Jacky spied the rescue ship, but the exhausted Kennedy could not bring himself to leave his horse and go through the mangroves on foot.

Sensing the time was right, a band of Aboriginal warriors attacked the fatigued men. Kennedy was struck by spears in the back, leg and side. Jacky was wounded above the eye but he did not leave his friend. Still surrounded by his attackers, Kennedy died in the weeping Jacky's arms. The words for the poem entitled 'In Jacky's own words' are taken verbatim from Jacky's account of Kennedy's last moments, as are the lines in 'Aftermath III'.

After Kennedy's death, Jacky hurriedly dug a shallow grave for him with his tomahawk, took up those of Kennedy's journals that he could carry, and made his way to the *Ariel*. It took him ten days, and he was stalked by hostile Aboriginal pursuers all the way. At one time he was forced to wade up to his neck in water to avoid them.

When he finally made it to the *Ariel*, Jacky and the crew rushed southwards to save the rest of the party. Nothing was found of the three men left behind by Jacky and Kennedy in their final dash for the sea. At Weymouth Bay only two of the eight men had survived – Mr Carron and one other man. Both men were skin and bone and near to death. Later search parties would be sent looking for Kennedy's remains but nothing of him was ever found.

---

2   Pudding Pan Hill in the Jardine River National Park.

An etching of the bewhiskered Kennedy, pencil in hand, slumped and dying in the arms of Jacky, would become a leitmotif of Australian exploration.

Jacky Jacky – the only member of the expedition to actually complete the journey – was awarded an inscribed bronze medallion for his bravery. He died years later, a forgotten man, of injuries sustained when he fell into a campfire.

How does it begin?

It begins with a swollen
Fragment of time,
An indrawn breath,

A young boy
On a misty island
Slipping

And falling.

It begins with a child's
Soft fingernails
Raking panic
Into cool green tree moss,

And a flash of leather sandal
And bony knees
Swirling through oak leaves.

It begins with an earthy thump
And a hot sudden exhalation,

The silence of the first shock
Eliding to a long teary wail,

And a small boy's realisation
That over-reaching
Can bring with it not just disaster,

But a flurry of petticoats also,
As anxious women rush from their kitchens
In the race to hold you tenderly
To their warm thighs and bosoms.

The Brisbane River

Dark thoughts
And shoulders stooped to a dull existence,

An Englishman
Reads a newspaper
Brought to him from the antipodes.

Fine New Holland dust
Yellows pages
Softened by humid tropical breezes.

Page One reports a body
Bloated beside the docks,
Shoes laced insouciantly around its neck,
And a mop of straw-blond hair.

A drowner.

Not uncommon on the lazy Brisbane River.
Drab and sensible from the banks
It will coolly take the weaker swimmer.

From another world
The Englishman,
Contemplating emigration,
Resents the mutterings of suicide.

He knows instinctively
The mind of the drowner –

As he waded into the murky water
And struck out for the other side,
As the currents took him
And swept him past tall cliffs
And drooping gums,
Even as his limbs grew tired
He was thinking:
    I am bigger than this
    And I can beat it.

Departure

It seems to Kennedy
That the whole ship is coughing softly
Into handkerchiefs.

A cargo of tubercular lungs
Slips with the currents
Down the Thames
And into its polluted estuaries.

Wisps of curious mist
Nudge the bow
And part for it,
Skimming across distant mudflats
Lightly,
Lazily.

Even in his thickest coat
Kennedy is cold
And shivering.
Becalmed for too long now,
He's keen to get on with it.

While others stand to aft
And wave weepily
At receding wharves
Kennedy sniffs the air for salt
And listens for the open sea.

When he remembers to look back
It's too late.
The fog has settled
And England is behind it,
Distant beyond reckoning.

When little waves slap the bow
At the place where
River first concedes to ocean,
Kennedy is too excited for second thoughts.

But as the ship begins to rear up
And lean into them,
And the mists clear
For the whirling gulls,
His breath catches for a moment
On the thought

That his mother back home
Moving back and forth
In her fireside rocking chair

And the timbers
Beneath his feet

Make the same forlorn
And weary creaking.

Circular Quay

First impressions are of quick blazes of white –
Sailors in the high rigging
Dodging puffs of cloud,

The starchy thwack of sails,

And squabbling gulls swooping
At the stinky fishguts
Bobbing on the rhythmic swell.

Kennedy is hot and frazzled
When he steps ashore
And looks up to find himself surrounded
By tall stacks of wicker cages,
And the hard screech and colour
Of scores of native birds.

It's a birder with his catch
Back from the interior,
Cashing in on the European taste
For pretty things
Encaged.
The man is thin and sun-red
And careless of their cries –
Four months in the dry country
Where branches laced with sticky resin
Catch as many as they slaughter.

A pair of green love birds
Rub peachy cheeks affectionately.
Tiny honey eaters
Flit anxiously from perch to perch.
But Kennedy is struck by the big black cockatoo –

Its dark intelligent eye,
The obscene flex of its crest,
The grey moistureless tongue
Rasping in the curved gaping beak,

And the great bird rocking
From side to side,
Weight shifting deliberately
One foot to the other,

Like a madman.

Encounter

From a squeaky carriage
On Tank Street,
Loaded down with baggage still smelling of
        England,
Kennedy sees his first Aborigines
Obliquely.

They settle awkwardly on his Old World memory,
If at all,
Like shadows.

One hour later
And he can call to mind no clear
Portrait of them

Though if pressed perhaps
He might say they had sagged a little

And huddled.

Letters of introduction

A neat pile of folded card
Tied with a white ribbon

Sees him alighting
From a hansom cab
One still evening

And standing uncertainly
At the bottom
Of a bank of sandstone steps –
Broad at the base,
Narrowing to a tall front door.

Ascending the steps
He sees in it all
Less a stately mansion
Than an immodest woman –
Legs spread sluttishly at hansom cabs
Rattling to a standstill
On dusty, rutted streets.

Blush

It does none of us any good –
Me unravelling like this
As if the release of my fist
At the handshake's close
Is the snag that undoes a knitted woollen.

Pink under my beard,
I struggle to meet their eyes,
While they respond to my shyness
With courtesy,
Even kindness,
And a hint of pity.

In a crowd of deep voices
And fat waistcoated bellies
I am such
A disappointment.

Dinner party

Loud chatter
Distorted by three quick scotches.

He's confounded by the laughter
And the swish of satin dresses.

When asked
He answers frankly:
   I am a surveyor.

He senses shutters closing politely
And bewhiskered merchants
With fat cigars
Thinking:
   This man can take me nowhere.

Learning the ropes

She is more uncertain than aloof.

The unexpected glide of his eyes
And her breasts cupped to a deep welcoming
    cleavage.

Her husband is getting the sherry
When she asks

And he says:
My father was the Mayor of London
And she surprises herself.

She wants him to make her laugh.

He is so pretty,
She is thinking.

The husband is introduced,
And a shy surveyor blushes
As he sips and thinks:

I would unfold this woman like a map.

At another time

A quiet man in a grey greatcoat,
Cowlick in his hair,
The scent of female high society
In his trousers,

Leaves by the tradesman's entrance.

Surveying

Standing naked
By the chaise longue

Feet together
Hands on hips

Her inner thighs touch
Along their length.

From his place between the pillows
It strikes him
That they form a line
Like a river's course

Diffusing
At the broad delta
Of her warm, luxuriant
Mons pubis.

Proving ground

When she said:
> *You take these things too seriously!*
> *I don't care if you see other women…*

He felt the world becoming
Something else –
Dimmer perhaps
And less kindly.

When he's told she's been seen in company
With a balding, middle-aged fool
He's aghast.

He imagines himself charging
Into battle –
Dropping the reins,
Head tilting back,
His chest exposed to the cannon.

Sydney City

Hunkered in fuggy rooms
Stale with rat droppings
And their own base stink

They seem content
To take it no further –

While I bide my time impatiently,
Breathless on the littoral of potential.

Arrivals

It's like kicking an ants' nest.

Watching from a distance
You see them swarming out,
In single file,
In leg irons,
Sickly and thin
And lungs moist with England.

They step ashore
Into the cry of invisible insects
As sharp
As a slap in the face.

(Odd that a scream
Can define the perfect silence.)

The light clarifying them.
The vastness absorbing them.

And the gum trees
Robed in teardrops.

I. An old convict recalls

The lash isn't so bad.

There's nothing as
Sincere as
Pain.

A lashed man
Is brought to a pitch
As perfect
As the cicada's shrill.

II. An old convict recalls

Levelling the ground
Where you now see George Street
We turned up dry old bones –
Blackfellas.

But nothing there for us.

No altars or henges.
Just blackfella bones
And the blank slate.

Frightening.

III. An old convict recalls

They found Georgey Henman
Propping up his back wall
With eighteen spears through his middle.
No steel.
No bronze.
No iron.
Just fire hardened wood
And the time to deliver eighteen of them.

Of course,
Time out there is a sharp flat horizon.

Eighteen was an arbitrary figure,
Settled on at leisure.

IV. An old convict recalls

No such thing as the convict stain
At first,
Because we all shared it
More or less.

That changed with the free settlers
And distinguished gents.

Hard work counts for nought
With a blunt hoe.

V. An old convict recalls

Six children out of eight
Is a good result.
One lost to measles
And the other to smallpox.

I buried them on the property.
My first declaration of permanence.

But one generation is not enough.
The graves of two small children
And a mottling of gum leaves
Says transience,
Not lasting.

Ringbarking is a better declaration.

Something permanent.
Eradication.

VI. An old convict recalls

When Maureen died with the ninth child
I felt it worse than ever.

Nothing cares as little
As a place without foundations.

I strode into the heat shimmers
And filled a deep silence with my anger.

With a bag of flour
And a flask of neat arsenic
I walked through tears to the waterhole
With my oldest motherless boy.

Bait them like dogs.
They can't resist the flour.
Watch the crows later from the homestead
Circling the cluster of she-oaks.

Other convicts know my meaning.

Those who have been hated
Learn first how to hate,
And only later,
Maybe,
Compassion.

Semantics

When he makes the high ground
Kennedy must pause,
Put down his case,
And pick out the furry grass seeds
Needling his long trousers.

He has attracted a band
Of naked black children –
All whispers, giggles,
Push and elbow.
They've politely kept him company
For a good ten minutes.

A minor commotion
And one skinny boy
Is pushed to the front of the little group.
He pipes up:
What you doin' mate?

Kennedy is about to answer
When another boy,
Frowning,
Chides his friend:
Hey!
Now you don't call him mate.
You call him mistah!

Testing the instruments

In the broad rural quiet
Kennedy can hear every chesty inhalation.

He is kneeling on the ground
Watched by his Pied Piper's band
Of black children.
They have no idea what's in the case
But even the youngest there
Senses its weighty importance.

When he takes out a set
Of tiny silver keys
The deft clockwise quarter-turn
Inspires an agony of anticipation.
Five-year-olds squirm
As if tickled by warm invisible fingers.

When Kennedy lifts the lid
And draws out his theodolite
(An oily gleaming instrument
All metallic precision)
A hush settles.
Some even shy away from it.

But every dark eye
Opens wide in amazement

And a pair of blue eyes also –
Kind and gentle,
Even reverent.
The children will say later
To disbelieving elders
Tugging their long white whiskers
In apprehension.

Jacky Jacky

You want his tribe?
You want his totem?
You want his blackfella name?

Well that's
None of your fucking business.

The water channel

Out here, the heat is a weight.

Spindly trees sag under it.
Silty dams and tepid reservoirs
Are smoothed glassy flat
By the burden of it.
Not a crease or ripple.
Like cotton submitting to the hot iron.

Out here
They speak of water with sexual longing.

Glen Ross Station.
Summer, 1847.
A child of two
Who has never smelt rain
Disengages himself from the cover
Of a latticed veranda
And on unsteady feet
Makes his way towards
A silver thread of water
Glistening behind the chicken sheds.

The water channel.
Twelve inches deep.

On either side,
Once-puddled earth
Has dried to fitted octagons.
The child totters.
Reverts to hands and knees.
Chubby pink palms press into the warm red dirt.

An outstretched hand,
A tentative fingertip,
Anticipating resistance.

And the surprise
As the membrane breaks –

The eyes screwed tight in reflex,
The lungful of stale liquid,
The angry bubbles in his ears
Fading
As dirty water settles again
To its own level.

And black crows in the treetops
Filling the still air
With their choking.

Provisions

Eight men
With hands in pockets
Regard a circle of yellow earth
Scalloped by the toes
Of their dusty leather riding boots.

Their lives have been refined
To a list of rations
Checked off
One by one
Against spheres of responsibility.

Flour?
   – *One ton.*
Tea?
   – *Ninety pounds.*
Sugar?
   – *Sixty pounds.*
Tents?
   – *Yes.*
Fishhooks?
   – *Yes.*
Niggers?

This one to Kennedy.

One,
He says,

One eye closed,
Tracing toe points
Dazily
With the tip of his index finger.

Shark attack

The mare's scent
Billowing in the water
Could only have been the scent of fear.

How else could the killer have discerned
Her unfamiliar
Chaffy, inland smell
As being from a thing
Both edible
And vulnerable?

We watched it all
From the safety of the ship's deck –
The harness snapping,
The belly splash,
The mare coming up swimming,
Her nostrils flared
And her sharp hooves striking at the brine.

And it occurred to me
That what makes the shark
So frightening and loathsome
Is both its clinical application
To the mechanics of slaughter
And its undignified loss
Of self-possession –

Who could watch
For more than a minute
As it hurled itself
At her big barrel body,
Grey back shuddering with the impact,
The blossom of blood,
And the dorsel fin circling
Like a rose thorn
Slicing the surface?

Sheep

Is there anything
So incongruous
As a fleecy sheep in mangroves
Blinking its delicate lashes?

We started with one-hundred sheep
And watched them die
Faster than we could eat them.

Dennis Dunn –
Our Irish Catholic –
Carries an image
In his breast pocket
Of the Saviour –

Impassive Christ
In monkish winter robes.
With one hand
He draws back the vestments.
With the other
He points to a radiant glowing heart.

This in the breast pocket
Of a sun-burned
Desiccated man
Wet with the sweat
Of tropical heat.

Dunn draws it out
From time to time
And presses it to his
Rosary-mumbling lips.

It's like leaving a dim room
For the bright glare of day.

I have been turning from Him.
He parches my throat.

Out here I find myself blinking,
And shading my eyes

From God.

Vines

This is weakness!

My petty
And delinquent mind
Conceding every night
To beautiful
Burdensome images
Of her soft bottom pressed to my thighs.

And in her locket
Nothing of me.

Leaving when more is left to say
Is like passing through
The rainforest again –

No horizon –

And the wait-a-while vines
Clutching

Beseeching me
With a thousand
Needy
Little fingers.

The hunt

Holding it before my face
As if it weren't a part of me,
I am regarding my own hand
In the grey of a cloudy dawn.

In an hour I will turn its form to slaughter.

Over my shoulder a conspiracy of whispers.
The camp is stirring
And other hands reach for weapons.

We are preparing for the hunt.

I turn it round slowly.
Front and back.
Blue veins.
White knuckles.
Callused palm.
It has gutted roos
And turned breasts taut with assent.

Slaughter and caress.

If I could devise such things
I would make a new religion.

I would worship hands.

Termite mounds

Our dark silhouettes –
A string of bedraggled
Bowed, defeated figures –
Pass now through a landscape
Of desolated sameness.

We have traded
The light-flattered
Shadow-patched
Barks and tendrils of the rainforest
For the open scrublands
And its heat shimmers,
Leaving us feeling
Vulnerable
And conspicuous.

We have passed up
The comforting intricacies of nature –
Lace-worked ferns,
Skeins of vine,
Tree trunks pinked with lichen –
For a place
With nothing to engage
Our troubled vision.

No heights to get our bearings,
We see our landmarks
Days in advance
Approaching at soul-destroying paces
And find them oddly,
When we reach them,
Much smaller than they had seemed.

Recalling the child
Hugging his knees
In his cosy cubby-house –
Two kitchen chairs
And a tent of blankets –
We crave at times,
Despite its humid toils,
The security provided
By the tangled canopy,
The tilted trunks,
The forest's arrogated
Manageable, modest
Horizons.

Instead we thread our way
Through fields of orange termite nests –
New Holland's obelisks,
Her broken columns.

But they give us little comfort –
Only a distance
And a middle distance,
A perspective with which to measure
The infinity of our woe.

Superiority

What language do we use
To persuade them
Of the grandeur of our venture

When all we have in gestures
Is our weepy sores
And pale ribs?

Our scientific weapons –
Calibrated on the killing fields
Of Borodino and Waterloo –

Mocked now from a distance
By bare black arses.

The horses

There's dear Mister Carron,
The Expedition botanist,
Shaking his head
And muttering,
>*Poor thing*
>*Poor thing*
And grimacing at the swing of the axe

But in the end
It was a relief.

We had shared the burden
Of growing thin together.

The final blow fell
Between sleepy, soft
Forgiving eyes.

I can still see
Poor Carron
Flinching

As we hunched our shoulders
To the task

Cracking open
Her elegant long bones
With hammers

In the hunt for
The rich dark marrow.

Botany

Mister Carron has been busy.

His gunny sack
Of seeds and nuts –
Filled over the weeks
In the interests of science –

Is emptied
Onto a white sheet
Spread out upon the ground
As if for a picnic.

He and Kennedy
And the helpful Jacky
Sort them all by type.

The men are gaunt
From toil and hunger.
Their stomachs rumble
With the potential at their toes.

Kennedy squats
With the other men
And takes up two nuts
In his tanned right hand.
He rattles them together
And gestures with his left:

Any of these good tucker, Jacky?

There is a hush of anticipation
As Jacky looks them over,
Brow furrowed with confusion.
He's almost crying
When he answers:

>   *I don't know Mister Kennedy.*
>   *This ain't my country.*

Those left behind

A small clearing
By a brackish waterhole

Flattered with yellow-white
Tropical sunlight

And dappled in places
By dark tree shadow.

Men lie sleeping
In contorted attitudes of dying –

Shallow breathing
Mouths agape –

A scene bleached of movement.

And not a sound,
Save the slow
Tink tink tink
Of a teaspoon
Stirring tannic water
In a battered billycan.

Inquiry

What you writin'
In them books Mister Kennedy?

Just words, Jacky.
Just words.

Campfire I

Watching Jacky's hands
As his shadow sets the fire
In the dull absences of the twilight
Is like watching
A flock of grey galahs wheeling
Against an overcast sky –

Light catching the underbellies
And the leaden clouds suddenly spotted
With flashes of unexpected colour.

He's picking up dry twigs
And gum leaves
For kindling
With both hands nimbly.
When he makes a joke
About my blistered bootless feet
I see the bright reassuring smile
Out of the black

And glimpses of fleshy pink
Which are his broad, sure
And gentle palms
Reaching out
In the darkness

And opening.

Campfire II

On a clear night you see
Whole constellations turning.

The black man is lying flat on the ground
Beneath a blanket,
One arm raised,
Forearm resting on his forehead.

The white man bends
Over the yellow glowing embers
And uses a knobby stick
To pull the billy from the coals.

Without turning
He asks kindly,
More tea Jacky?

The black man yawns
And stretches,
Yes please, Mister Kennedy.

A mug of hot sweet tea
Passes in the darkness.

Journal keeping

Kennedy closes his journal
And sighs
As if he has lowered
A great weight to the ground.

He's sitting with his back
Against a tree
And with his knees drawn up.
He lowers his head to them,
Eyes closed.

Jacky glances up.

> *You been writin' more of them words*
> *Mister Kennedy?*

He nods.

> *No wonder you're buggered.*

Quarry

It's not the fox
Evading hounds.

There's no cunning double-back
Or clever hidey-place

And the hounds don't chase.

The blackfellas follow casually
Out of spear-range,
Miming our anguished
Spear-stuck deaths
With weapons held to their own necks
And melodramatic eye-rolling.

The shadows in the shadows
Compound the indignity
Of our clumsy shambling
With dark observant eyes,
Jeers and laughter

And as the night descends,
With hurled stones
And rustles in the scrub.

So much space.
Why all the spear-shaking?

Invaders

Hours after sundown
The breezes shift
And the sounds of distant corroboree
Settle lightly on their blankets
As they doze.

A dry branch snapping
And the thump of bare feet running
Sees them reaching frantically
For cold gun barrels.

Then no more singing,
And a great ponderous stillness.
Total.

Just as two people sitting quietly
Can never be as silent
As a crowd of hushed thousands.

Journal entry I

Nothing is as still
As the weary gum
In summer.

Nothing except
Maybe the natives
Stalking roos.

Shadows halting –
One foot raised midstep –
And the trees,
The roos,
The blacks,
All competing for stillness.

Only the cicadas agitating.
A continent holding its breath.

Journal entry II

This is no place for passion.

Lie back under a shady tree
And watch the slow arc
Of eagles
Wheeling through heat shimmers.

When it drops from the sky
To seize its prey,
The eagle does so
Without anger
Or venom.

Perched on a dead branch
With a writhing animal
In its sure talons,
The coup de grace,
The feeding,
Strikes it as an afterthought.

The eagle is unhurried
By the pain at its clawtips.

I can't help but feel
That we have been
A little too hasty,

Impatient in a place
That has nothing to do
But wait.

Journal entry III

It is the hunt
That manifests our differences.

I raise my shotgun
And train the sights
On a flock of cockatoos
Resting in a spindly gum.

The report
Sends a white sheet
Of wild screeches
Beating into the blue sky.

Haste.
Peace shattered.
And nothing to show for it.

This place

The scrublands don't bar our egress
If by 'barring'
We imply some active hostility.
This place bears us no ill will.

A clue to our significance
Lies in the broad shoulders
Of the Pacific
Shrugging indifferently.

I have been searching for a word
That says what this place is,
And I think that it might be
Something like
The opposite of fervour.

If it rains tomorrow
And saves a ragged band
Of thirsty men
It will only be rain.
The rest will be incidental.

What are we to make of it?

We walk these days
Through great vastnesses
Without words.
I find myself doing so
With a peculiar wistfulness
Akin to nostalgia

Knowing that movement
Towards something
Must also mean movement
Away from things.

Journal entry IV

Just me and Jacky left now.
Enfeebled.

Alone
But not entirely
Lonely.

Stumble

A front of smouldering scrub fires
Smuts the air
And sets the hollowed eyes
Of two scabbed
And famished men
To stinging.

Two tiny
Urgent figures
In a scalding white landscape,

Stumbling dumbly
From nothingness
To nothingess,

Overwhelmed
By enormous
Dimensionless spaces.

They stagger desperately into emptiness,
Hurrying to fill it,
Allured by some infinite craving.

One man falls,
Gets up,
And then the other.

Too tired to speak.

Supporting, friendly hands reach out
As in a dream,

Sometimes white
And sometimes black.

Pudding Pan Hill

Standing alone
On the high ground –
A flat-topped hill
Like an upturned pudding pan –
Jacky can see
The bright
White sails of the rescue ship
Catching the morning sun.

He calculates
That a healthy man
Might traverse the scrub
And mangroves
Falling between them
In just a few days.

He returns to the campsite
In long loose strides.

He finds Kennedy
Lying on his side,
Asleep across his saddlebags,
Firearm slipped from his fingers,
Jaundiced-yellow
And whiskery.

He is dying.

The white man barely stirs at first.
With help, he raises himself
Onto one elbow.

Thank God you came back, Jacky

Murmurs Kennedy
(He's cradled in Jacky's arms now,
Head nestled against his chest).
He touches Jacky's forearm softly.

I missed you.

The last hurdle

To Jacky
Their knock-kneed nags
Had never seemed so
Big and weighty
As in those last few days
When harried by blacks
They had tripped through
The tangle of mangroves
For the rescue ship.

He saw in their
Mean little hooves
Sinking in the mud
Impediments,
And in their ribbed chests
Broad targets for spears.

But when Jacky said

> *We should leave the horses, boss.*
> *We can walk to the coast,*

The exhausted Kennedy
Fell back on a deep European instinct –
A settled, domesticated
Agrarian meme –
And refused him without thinking.

He registered it
At the gut level
As a forsaking
Of rights hard won –

The abandonment of bloodlines
Distilled by generations
Of stolid, callus-palmed
Breeders and cultivators.

We will stay with the horses,

Said Kennedy,
Though Jacky had dismounted.
Standing with the reins
In his hands
He regarded the white man
Slumped in the saddle,

Horse and rider
Bonded by weariness,
Heads and shoulders dipped by fatigue.

Jacky knew then that Kennedy
Would die out there
With lessons left to learn

While he
Perhaps
Might make it.

The attack

When it finally comes
It's almost welcome.

The only hasty
Panicked part

The whistle of a few spears.

In Jacky's own words

I told him
Blackfellows always die
When he got spear wound in there.

He said:
> *I am out of wind, Jacky.*

I asked him:
> *Are you going to leave me?*

And he said:
> *Yes, my boy,*
> *I am going to leave you.*

> *I am very bad, Jacky.*

> *You take the books.*

Last words

The pencil in his clumsy fingertips
Seems huge and heavy –

The only solid
Sensible thing
In a world grown soft
And insubstantial.

He has the sensation
That it's all disintegrating
At some impossible
Molecular level –

Rending softly along threadlines
Like worn out fabric.

He sees each grain of sand
Like some giant
Worthy
Sculpted thing –

But Jacky's voice
Seems wind-distorted,
Diminished,
Diluted by a distance
Of a thousand miles.

He feels the nausea of a great loss,
Is lulled by the sibilants of falling rain.

He reaches for words
As liquid as tepid water
(The many things he'd like to say).

He's fading and falling
As he begins to write

I am sorry
If I let you down.

Ghost armies

Our battles generally
Have been modest affairs
Fought desultorily,
And never en masse.

The notion of a cavalry charge
Across the saltpan
Or cannon ranged
Beneath the boughs
Of the paperbark
Strikes us as vaguely ridiculous –
Overtly epic
In the circumstances.

No farmer's wife
Ever woke here at night
To the tramp and dust
Of eerie ghost armies
Marching to war,
To death,
Beneath her window sill.

We look elsewhere
For our bloodbaths.

Our war cries have
Typically been attenuated
By great distances.
The raised voices
Of our desperation
Might be easily mistaken
For the sound of young men
Behind the branding yards

Chiacking.

An epilogue

This is too muted,
Surely, to be termed
A homecoming.

Two men stretchered
Quietly and gently
Down a gangway
As time slows,
Eddies and pools
Like the current
Of a grand river.

They are taken to a dockside shed
Where they will be reunited
With wives and children
In scenes tinted to sepia
By the play of slanted light
On pollen-laden air.

A swirl of motes.
This is the sickly colour
Of pity.
Its sound
Is that of grown men
Murmuring softly amongst themselves
With their agitated eyes
Cast down.

One of the men –
Sweetly odorous,
Near to death –
Is Mister Carron.
His bruised and sunken eyes
Do not open
As they ease him down
With exaggerated care.
He lies there
On his stretcher,
On the floor,
His tremulous eyelids flittering.

An awkward half-minute passes
Under the covetous
Patient gaze of death.

The door opens.
Three women swoop in
And move to Carron swiftly.
A daughter to each hand
And his wife to his pallid forehead

And it seems to the embarrassed bystanders
That they settle about him
On their skirted knees
As lightly and as gracefully
As a linen sheet
Cast out from the body
During bed-making,
Anchored by a hemline,
And air-buoyed
Drifting to the mattress.

Such tenderness!
They press warm lips to his skin.
They stroke his hands softly.

Poor Carron.
Botanist.
More dead than alive.

He stirs.
He opens his eyes.

Aftermath I

Returning weeks later,
They found no bones
To mark his passing.
Poor tear-worn Jacky
Could only approximate the spot –

Some gently sloping ground
Like any other,
And clusters of grass-trees
Shimmering in the humid breezes.

Here Jacky?
Here?

Would-be cairn builders
Frustrated by Jacky's anxious head scratching.

Aftermath II

It's more than likely that
As Jacky fled
Through the spiny, lacerating scrub
For the cool antisepsis
Of the bright, surging ocean

They dug him up again –

Jacky's shallow, tomahawked grave
No impediment –

And turned him over,
To lie face down,
So the cheeks of his white arse
Were showing.

Aftermath III

I was crying a good while
Until I got well.

How does it end?

At night

No part of a country town
Is darker
Than the dry riverbed
On its fringes

Where bottles pass
From hand to hand
Across emberbeds
Burning low and red.

Where anger flares.

And where the first feather-touch
Of yellow flame
On skin

Can feel as cool
As polished bronze.

www.ingramcontent.com/pod-product-compliance
Lightning Source LLC
Chambersburg PA
CBHW051843090426
42736CB00011B/1929